Creatures
Close Up

Gillian Watts

Photographs by
Philippe Martin

This small Mediterranean **ringed millipede** lives under stones in dry places. It has 16 legs and eats plant litter. When it is disturbed, it rolls into a ball. Philippe was looking for a scorpion under some stones when he found this tiny living sphere—only about 1/4 inch (5 mm) across.

Creatures Close Up

Gillian Watts

Photographs by

Philippe Martin

FIREFLY BOOKS

A FIREFLY BOOK

Published by Firefly Books Ltd. 2016
Copyright © 2016 Firefly Books Ltd.
Text copyright © 2016 Gillian Watts
Photography copyright © 2016 Philippe Martin

First printing

Publisher Cataloging-in-Publication Data (U.S.)
Names: Watts, Gillian, author. | Martin, Philippe, 1954-, photographer.
Title: Creatures close-up / author, Gillian Watts; photographer, Philippe Martin.
Description: Richmond Hill, Ontario, Canada : Firefly Books, 2016. | Includes index | Summary: "Skilled photographer Philippe Martin, compiles his high-focused pictures of bugs, arachnids, birds, reptiles, and amphibians in nature, to inspire the next generation to take up a camera and capture incredible photos of their own. The book is mainly high definition photos with captions about the animal, perfect for young readers" – Provided by publisher.
Identifiers: ISBN 978-1-77085-782-7 (paperback) | 978-1-77085-783-4 (hardcover)
Subjects: LCSH: Photography of animals – Juvenile literature. | Animals — Pictorial works — Juvenile literature. | Photography, Close-up – Juvenile literature.
Classification: LCC TR727.W388 |DDC 778.324 – dc23

Library and Archives Canada Cataloguing in Publication
Martin, Philippe, 1954-, photographer
Creatures close-up / Philippe Martin, photographer ; text by Gillian Watts.
Includes index.
ISBN 978-1-77085-783-4 (hardback).—ISBN 978-1-77085-782-7 (paperback)
1. Wildlife photography—Juvenile literature. 2. Animals—Pictorial works—Juvenile literature. 3. Photography, Close-up--Juvenile literature. I. Watts, Gillian, writer of added text II. Title.
TR729.W54M37 2016   j779'.32   C2016-902267-6

Published in the United States by
Firefly Books (U.S.) Inc.
P.O. Box 1338, Ellicott Station
Buffalo, New York 14205

Published in Canada by
Firefly Books Ltd.
50 Staples Avenue, Unit 1
Richmond Hill, Ontario L4B 0A7

Cover and interior design: Janice McLean

Printed in China

The publisher gratefully acknowledges the financial support for our publishing program by the Government of Canada through the Canada Book Fund as administered by the Department of Canadian Heritage.

Dedication

To Frédéric Melki, longtime naturalist friend,
and Frédéric Jaulmes, master of image and light.

—P. M.

To Robert Barnett, husband and photographer
par excellence.

—G.W.

About the Photographer

Philippe Martin is a naturalist and photographer who lives in the south of France, near the Mediterranean Sea. He has been taking photographs for 40 years, but he developed his "Hyper Focus" technique just recently. He first used this process to photograph animals and plants in the area where he lives.

In 2013 Philippe went to Madagascar, a huge island nation off the southeast coast of Africa. The island is home to thousands of animal species that are found nowhere else. Philippe spent 28 days in the rainforest there and took 100,000 pictures! Many of the images in this book come from that "mission impossible," as he calls it.

The Madagascar hedgehog

is not really a hedgehog at all, but a small mammal called a tenrec. It can often be seen moving through the plants growing on the forest floor.

This small **fish** comes from a forest stream in Madagascar. Its species is still unknown.

Hyper Focus photographs can be taken underwater. The photo on opposite page was taken using this camera setup.

Close-up Photography

Photography is like painting with light. The lens — the "eye" of the camera — controls the light that goes inside the camera, where the image is captured and preserved. Before digital photography was invented, this image was captured on film, which then had to be developed and printed. Now it is captured electronically and stored as a computer file, which can be printed or viewed on a monitor.

How much light enters our eye is controlled by its pupil. This is the black hole in the center of the eye that gets larger and smaller, depending on how much light there is. The camera lens can be adjusted in much the same way. How widely it opens is called its aperture (meaning "opening"), and that controls how much light is used to make the image.

Making pictures with a camera also involves two other important elements: shutter speed and focus. The shutter is a cover behind the lens that keeps light out of the camera until you're ready to take a picture. When you hear a camera click, that's the shutter opening and closing to make a single exposure. The faster the shutter clicks, the easier it is to "freeze" motion, which is especially important when photographing animals. The shutter is open for only a fraction of a second, but you can make many exposures very quickly. You have probably heard this happening on TV, when famous people are being photographed by news reporters.

When an object is in focus, it looks very sharp and clear. Our eyes are constantly changing their focus on the things around us — it's an automatic process that we usually don't notice.

Shooting in an outdoor mini studio. A small reflector and diffuser soften and even out the sunlight.

A camera can focus on a very small portion of an object or, if you want, a much bigger part of it. The size of the area that's in focus depends on what is called depth of field. This zone of sharp focus is controlled by how wide open the lens is. The smaller the aperture (lens opening), the greater the depth of field.

When you get very close to something, it is hard to focus on it. (Try this with a finger in front of your face.) This becomes a problem in macro-photography, the term for extreme close-ups. To get a sharp picture, you need a small aperture. But that means less light can get into the camera, so you have to keep the shutter open longer. The longer the shutter is open, the more chance there is that the subject will move or the camera will jiggle. Result — a blurry picture. Read on to find out how Philippe solved this problem.

The Hyper Focus Process

To get all of your subject in a picture, normally you move the camera further back. But then you lose the valuable details that macrophotography reveals. To capture the amazing features of tiny animals and plants, you need to get very close to your subject. But when the camera is that close, the zone of sharp focus is reduced to only a few millimeters. To solve this problem, Philippe Martin invented the Hyper Focus process.

In the first part of the process, he takes dozens of photographs of his subject, each focused on a different part of it. Watching Philippe at work is fascinating. First he finds a good background for the animal, such as a flat rock or low branch. Then he sets up a reflector — a piece of white cardboard on a mini tripod — which helps even out the light. He gently captures his tiny subject and sets it on the background. Then he gets his camera as close as possible to it and starts shooting. The shutter goes click-click-click — faster than you can count — while Philippe smoothly turns the lens, constantly changing its focus.

After he has taken the pictures, Philippe downloads them to his computer. The next step in the process uses something called focus-stacking software. This program looks at all the photos and finds the parts of each one that are in perfect focus. It then joins together all those perfectly focused parts to make one composite image — a picture in which the whole subject is in perfect focus.

Focus-stacking software works best with very small subjects. This is because changing the focus with each shot also changes the angle of view a little. When the software puts all the exposures together, problems can result, such as a blurry halo around the subject. So the Hyper Focus process also includes erasing such problems, one by one, using image-processing software such as Photoshop. This "digital painting" can take hours, but the result is a stunning image that tells us a great deal about its subject.

The outdoor mini studio has been set up. The camera is on a heavy, stable mount a few centimeters from the subject. Then Philippe starts taking pictures in "multi-capture" mode. From the first to the last shot, he must not move the camera or the subject. This is the first photograph in a series of a dung beetle — only the tip of the insect's "horn" is in focus. Sixty-five mostly blurry photos later, this is the resulting composite image.

The **rainbow bush locust**, one of the "gaudy grasshoppers," is limited to certain regions in Madagascar. Some people consider it to be the most beautiful grasshopper in the world. Its relatives can be found in Australia.

This startled-looking insect is a type of **praying mantis** found in Madagascar. It uses its strong front legs to capture other insects and even small lizards and frogs.

This female **bloody-nosed beetle** was photographed in a lightbox. Its name comes from its habit of producing a nasty-tasting red liquid from its mouth when threatened.

The **yellow-tailed scorpion** is common in southern France and is sometimes found in houses. Although it looks quite scary, it is only about 1½ inches (35–45 mm) long.

This large Mediterranean **land snail** is about 2 inches (4–6 cm) long.
The image shows the dark blue color of the snail's body as it crawls along the damp ground.

The **lined day gecko** comes in many colors and patterns. This beautiful lizard is native to Madagascar and has become popular as a pet in North America.

The **common brown lemur** is found in Madagascar and on Mayotte, a small island nearby. This was a captive animal, which is how Philippe was able to get such a good image.

The **garden dormouse** is found in various parts of Europe, where it builds a globe-shaped nest of grass and moss in bushes and trees. It sleeps during the day and comes out at night to look for food.

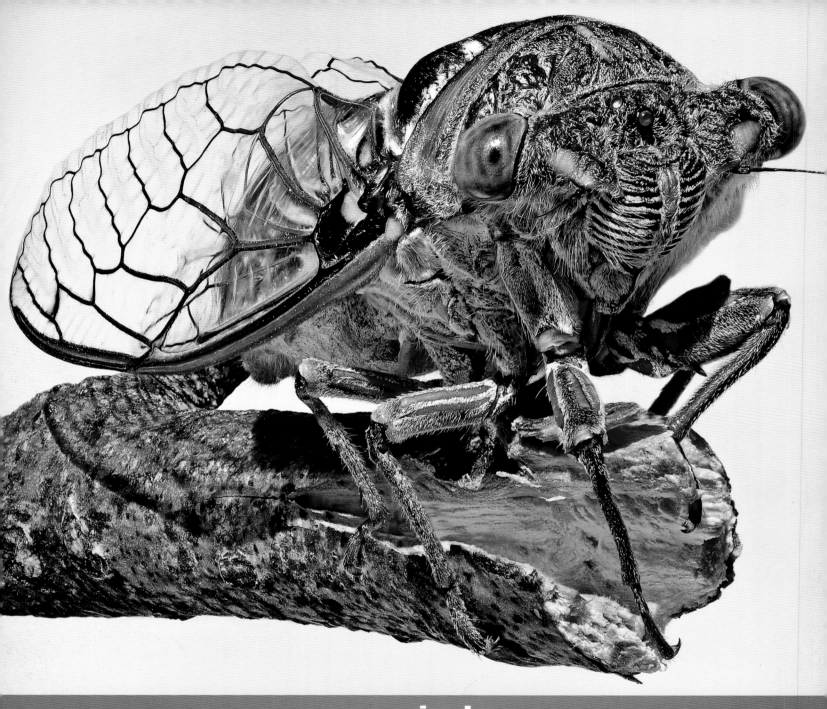

A female common **cicada** spreads its wings on a late June morning, just after changing from a larva into an adult. The three red dots on its head are called simple eyes, or ocelli. The insect uses them to detect movement.

This bristly insect is a large **June bug** that is common in Madagascar. A tiny spider is crashing the photo (below the bug's back leg).

23

The **western green lizard** is found in Europe from northern Spain to Serbia, and in the United States. During spring courtship, its throat turns bright blue.

This giant tropical **millipede** from Madagascar eats things it finds on the forest floor. It has no fangs, but it can squirt a poisonous spray that will kill small animals such as frogs.

The caterpillar of the **giant peacock moth** — the largest moth in Europe — ranges in color from yellow to green to dark orange. This one is ready to spin its cocoon and begin the final stage of becoming an adult.

This small female **fly** — less than ¼ inch (4 mm) long — is notable for its very large compound eyes.

The **rose chafer** is a metallic-looking green beetle. It feeds on pollen, nectar and flowers — particularly roses — in many parts of Europe.

Pygora beetles — also called flower beetles — are small, colorful insects with a metallic sheen. They are native to Madagascar.

This **harbor crab**, also called a sandy swimming crab, was photographed on France's Mediterranean coast. It grows to only 2 inches (5 cm) across.

The small **Tsarafidy Madagascar frog** is related to the golden mantella frogs on pages 42 and 43. Like its cousin, it is found only in Madagascar. It lives in forests and swamps. Also like its cousin, it is threatened by habitat loss.

33

This is a
European rhinoceros beetle —
the reason for its name is clear! Only the males have horns, which they use to fight over females. The winner is the beetle that flips its opponent off the branch they are fighting on.

A **golden silk orb-weaver** seen from below. This male spider is particularly colorful.

Argiope spiders are known for having a colorful abdomen. This one, from Madagascar, is sitting in the shelter of a rock in an open area near its large, globe-shaped web.

This beautiful adult
fire salamander
broke the record for time spent
being photographed. For two full
days in the fall, it never moved
from where it was sitting.

The family of this **net-winged owlfly** can be recognized by their bulging eyes and the knobs on their antennae. They fly over grassy areas in search of other insects to eat.

This giant **fly** — it's 1½ inches (4 cm) long — is a member of the "robber fly" family. It kills other insects by stabbing them with its stiff, sharp proboscis, which works like a hypodermic needle to suck up their insides.

This **variegated golden frog**, also known as Baron's mantella, was photographed in the rain. One of the most colorful small amphibians in Madagascar, its survival is threatened by habitat loss. (The bright yellow background is a dead leaf at the edge of a stream.)

The **golden mantella** is a rare frog found only in Madagascar forests. A major conservation program has been set up to protect this endangered species.

A **stick insect** (also known as a walking-stick) pretends to be a twig. This clever camouflage method protects it from predators.

44

A large
orb-weaving spider
on a carpet of moss.
This type of spider is
often found at the
edges of forests
in Madagascar.

Wolf spiders are skilled hunters with excellent eyesight — note the two very large eyes above four smaller ones. After their eggs hatch, they carry around the larvae for several days. (Yes, those are baby spiders on the abdomen of this female.)

The male **comet moth** is one of the largest insects in the world, with a wingspan of almost 8 inches (20 cm). It lives in the rainforests of Madagascar.

A large male **Escher's blue butterfly** drinking on wet mud at the edge of a pond. Philippe had to keep moving the Hyper Focus mini-studio to stay close enough to it.

This giant **leafhopper** from Madagascar is 1 inch (3 cm) long. If you look closely, you can see delicate, sensitive bristles at the ends of its antennae.

This tiny, tank-like insect is one of thousands of species of **weevil**. Philippe found this one in Madagascar.

The **Madagascar tree boa** is impressively long — up to 7 feet (2 m). It is also the only boa constrictor Philippe has met that didn't try to bite him. Perhaps this is because it has no enemies where it lives.

This young bird — a
black redstart —
settled down for about
10 seconds in front of Philippe's
window in France before
flying off to new
adventures.

54

This strange-looking object is a pupa of the **lime hawk-moth**. It will spend the winter in the ground and then hatch into a large and very handsome moth.

This beautiful animal is a female **Madagascar bright-eyed frog**. These frogs can be found moving through the forest almost every night. They are threatened by habitat loss.

The **brown leaf chameleon** lives on a small island near Madagascar. It hides from enemies by disguising itself as a dead leaf. This photo shows chameleons' amazing ability to move their eyes separately and in every direction.

This **longhorn beetle** makes up for its tiny size with handsome red-and-white elytra, or hardened wing covers.

The **mossy leaf-tailed gecko** of Madagascar is a master of camouflage. It normally lives on tree trunks covered in lichen.

This **frog** from Madagascar is an expert at camouflage. It blends right into its swampy habitat.

61

This is the larva of a
conehead mantis,
which is a kind of praying mantis
found near the Mediterranean Sea.
Young mantises look like a dead twig,
but the adults are bright green —
more like a piece of grass.

Index